2017

THE RECESSION

Just hours before the Titanic sank the sailors were excited of being in such an engineering marvel of its time.

Mar 23 2016

Credit Suisse announced that it plans to fire 6000 of its employees. Year To Date 2800 terminated.

Mar 30 2016

A steel major announced exit from Britain. 15,000 jobs on the line...

40,000 more jobs affected.

Oct 21 2016

Deutsche Bank

The US DOJ slaps a fine of 14 billion dollars on Deutsche bank. Stock of Deutsche Bank touches single digit.

9000 jobs on the line

Nov 05 2016

Marks And Spencer

Shuts Down 10,20,30,40,50,60,70,80,90... 100 Stores.

Trump Elected President of America

Nov 15 2016

France Prime Minister

" Europe On Brink Of Collapse"

It's Right Here. Facing You.

2017

The Recession

COPYRIGHT@DR.RAVINHUMBARWADI

PIAM CREATIONS

Reach Out To Me : pi.con.publisher@gmail.com

ONLY YOU CAN ACT.

A bit in the beginning of 2016. By the end of 2016 the crisis will be out in the open. Early 2017 the situation worsens, only to hit the lowest point in mid - late 2017. We will be a mute witness to the spectacle of an economic holocaust.

Cause and effect. Indicators and outcome. This is the an economic diagnosis done on the basis of an analysis of the symptoms. Everything is open in front of you and as you turn page after page you can see your collective economic destinies unfold before your eyes.

Wear your logic and analyze. Everyone can reach a conclusion. I have reached a conclusion. You read and decide.

YOU CAN ACT ONLY IF YOU KNOW.

Early Warning : Stay Alert. Early Warning : Stay Alert.

One thing will shock you – the speed. Fast and furious. It gives you no second chance.

From now on economy as life will have to be managed with an eye on cause and effect. Whatever we do will comeback to us with a multiplier.

Early Warning Stay Alert.

The Global Economic Crisis Simplified. So You Know What To Do.

What Can You Do Now ?

Nobody Will Act For You.

Each One For Himself. Each One For Herself.

THE COMING CRASH

On February 12 2016 as I write this, the world witnessed just the beginning of the great fall that will culminate in an economic disaster.

On February 11 2016 Janet Yellen chaired a meet of the US Federal Reserve. During the meet, news channels were abuzz - 'China faced its worst year of economic growth in a quarter century. Oil went down again putting a question mark on the oil centric economies of Russia, Brazil and the Middle East. Wall Street closed to the worst ever start to a year.'

Gold spiked. The safe haven.

This is what has happened. I will now tell you what will happen and how you can mitigate the effect and take precautions so that you don't end up on the wrong side of the biggest economic disaster in your lifetime.

Watch out for the 3 dates with destiny. In the last month of 2016 we will enter the last lap of a familiar terrain. The first dip to signal the start. From then on we will be holding on to straws to escape the cyclonic winds of an economic downturn out in the open. In the beginning of 2017 the second fall will confirm our worst fears. In the last quarter of 2017 the third fall will enter 2017 in history books as the year when the global economic recession happened.

Exactly a century back we had the World War 1. Will the cataclysmic event a century later be an economic depression? An economic holocaust perhaps. Because this time the indicators are gigantic in proportion.

The Gold Surge.

On 11 Feb 2016 the stocks fell and gold spiked. Imagine the spike when the market fall is 5 times more. The spike will be proportionate. Gold will again spike in Dec 2016.

Feb 2016

News: Stocks are down in the dumps the world over. It was a catastrophic night. And going by the early signs, it won't be a pretty morning as markets are sliding again...

News: Worldwide stocks stumbled on fears over the health of the global economy. The global equity benchmark index closed more than 20 per cent below its record high in 2015.

An all-country world equity index, which tracked shares in 45 nations hit its lowest level in more than two and a half years.

Nature has given us many years and more opportunities to take effective action. But when we don't, it steps in and makes sure we pay for the economic blunders we have committed.

In 2116 historians may well point back at those who managed the global economy in the first two decades of this century; those who imagined they could trick people and nature. Or did they really believe that their action was the answer to combat the 2008 recession. Let's check out how they messed up our finances!

China, USA, Europe, Japan and Middle East. Let's journey.

The Great Fall Of China

Let's begin with China. Because this is where it all began.

Problems arising from China have globally crashed stock and commodity markets.

The iron ore that China gulped from Rio de Janeiro to Australia was used to build mega fetal cities. The 'fetal - unborn cities' that became infamous across the globe as the 'ghost cities of China'. The world's second biggest economy built cities after cities, hundreds of them but not a single person chose to stay.

Unborn, unused and unusable. Homes, restaurants, malls, gladiatorial stadia that should have been bustling with vibrant people were mute witness to empty space.

It took some time before the world became aware of this. It seemed more fictional than truth.

China's 'infrastructure' driven growth of two decades costed billions and led to a cascading worldwide boom starting off with commodity prices.

Were the 'unborn cities' at the core of this global boom?

Tremendous money had gone in but resulted in no output making these the debt cities of China.

The showpiece of an economic boom was just dead weight in the sinking ship of China and the global economy.

Somewhere the cities had to stop because they were lying empty. And when it did the commodities that went into the making of the cities crashed. As much as 50 % - 80% and more.

The debt was funded by bonds, many of which were collateralized with copper. And copper was down. So neither was there a ROI nor was there value in the collateral. Debt recovery was a distant dream.

More the debt, more the trouble. We all want to hide our debts. But sooner or later it will come out in the open. Then all mayhem breaks loose. Like it did in Feb 2016.

The Chinese economy posted growth of 6.9% in 2015, its slowest rate since 1990. China's forex reserves are down by a whopping 700 billion dollars. The Dec 2015 manufacturing PMI revealed a sluggish industrial production for the 10th consecutive month. No wonder then, in Feb 2016 Chinese equity markets went into a downslide.

Marc Faber, the author of 'Gloom and Doom Report' says that 'the Chinese economy was heading for a hardlanding, as borrowers piled up debt and were finding it difficult to pay interest.'

George Soros stated that the current Chinese situation "amounts to a crisis" and brings memories of the recession of 2008. "China is struggling to find a new growth model and its currency devaluation is transferring problems to the rest of the world." Soros has blamed the Chinese economy for global bearishness.

Commodity expert Jim Rogers: "The US stock market was down last year. This started in the US and Europe. China is just catching up in a big-big way."

China is releasing huge cash into its financial system in an effort to stem the tide. But you cannot treat a cancer with a placebo.

The Chinese fear a quick devaluation of their currency.

The last time China devalued Renminbi, it caused the Asian currency crisis.

China challenges a currency trader. Not to bet against the Renminbi.

George Soros may be legendary.

Yet you are left with a niggling thought: The mighty colossus challenges a mere trader! Why should a colossus even acknowledge let alone take cognizance of a trader of currencies.

Because it is afraid. Yes. China is scared!

China is scared because it is unfolding and doesn't know what to do.

As of October 2016 the credit to GDP gap is at 30% when 10% is the highest as per international norms.

'China is in the midst of a triple bubble, with the third-largest credit bubble of all time, the largest investment bubble and the second-largest real-estate bubble.' This is a Credit Suisse analysis.

In 1992, George Soros became known as the man who "broke" the Bank of England. He gained $1 billion betting that the pound would collapse.

What do you think George Soros has done in 2016?

He has bet against Asian currencies and commodity linked economies.

Now, one Mr. Donald Trump is the President of USA.

Ding Deng.

China Is Unfolding. Stay Alert.

USA Uncertain

Feb 11 2016. Janet Yellen at a Fed meet accepted that if the recent dire global economic indicators continued it could be multiplying downside risk to the USA.

The unemployed and the not so well employed number in the USA is an election issue and these form the swell of support to Trump, the unlikely candidate. This is well known. Americans in large numbers do not have enough savings in their bank account.

What is the reason for this situation that USA finds itself in?

There were three rounds of quantitative easing (QE). QE1 was from 2008 to 2010. The US Fed bought $2.1 trillion of treasury bonds and mortgage-backed securities. This stopped when the Fed indicated that there was improvement in the economy.

But the recovery proved to be false. So QE 2 was on. It started in November 2010 and lasted till the middle of 2011. During QE2 the US Fed bought $600 billion of bonds comprising mostly mortgage-backed securities.

After a little more than a year the Fed realized there was no real recovery.

So it started QE3 in late 2012 and during this program the Fed pumped in $85 billion per month. The Fed began reducing those purchases at the start of 2015.

The Fed has spent more than $4 trillion in buying bonds.

There is a broad consensus that QE1 was a success - it was quite big: a couple of trillion dollars, and lasted quite long: a couple of years. It helped in preventing the 2008 recession becoming worse than it was.

QE2 was only a third as effective as QE1. The San Francisco Federal Reserve Bank, found that QE2 added just 0.13 percentage points to the annual rate of economic growth in 2010, which was at 2.8% when the program was implemented.

The Fed had a prolonged QE3. And it would prove to be the unwanted QE. The QE that did the damage. The QE that disrupted the caravan.

Money at low rates leads to speculation. It would be a fallacy to think that highs of the US stock markets are not in large measure due to the QE.

Now that the QE is not there where do you imagine the US stocks are headed? How long will the markets sustain?

Just stand back and take a quick look, do a quick think.

Because there is not much time left to get out of the stock market.

Andrew, a former manager of the Fed's mortgage-buying scheme, has commented that low rates may not have helped ordinary Americans.

Was Wall Street sucking in most of the extra cash?

Greed. The greed of Wall Street. But then a cardinal sin never goes without leaving a trail and retribution. Does it? The time is near. The time has arrived.

Printing money in the world's biggest economy also had an impact on global economies.

The European Central Bank, found that QE1 and QE2 led to spillovers in as many as 65 economies across the globe.

The study revealed that QE1 led investors to invest in USA while QE2 led investment into emerging economies. Now, that source of easy money is shut and scores of countries are feeling the 'Easy Money Withdrawal Syndrome.' The tap is dry and they are feeling blanked out.

A lot of Americans want Donald Trump as president. Would he have this support if the situation had been different. Yes, terrorism apart has not the state of the economy led a large section of the people to look towards someone like Trump to spruce up the system in Washington ?

Hillary Clinton may be the bettor's choice but Trump is a creation of his times. And creation of the times however eccentric have been known to be unusually powerful.

Ben Bernanke spent $3 trillion to make the NYSE a bull market for half a dozen years. Janet Yellen hiked the interest rate by a quarter point and the bull market tanked by a third of its value.

So weak is the stock market.

In September 2016 the Fed once again postponed the itsy bitsy rate hike. It looked so huge, so gargantuan. Given the weak signals continuing to emanate from the economy.

What about the rate hike in December 2016?

If the Fed does increase the interest rate it will be the straw that broke the camel's back. The stockmarket will come crashing down.

The great depression of 2017 would be all out there. And Fed will be trying to save themselves being blown away.

The fragile economy has left no one to bold enough to bite the bullet.

"The world is an uncertain place, and all monetary policymakers can really be sure of is that what will happen is often different from what we currently expect." Stanley Fischer, the No. 2 at the U.S. Federal Reserve.

USA Uncertain...

Europe Lives In Delusion

Feb 2016 News: 'SocGen leads European banks lower at the close as Deutsche, Barclays, HSBC, Lloyds and RBS share prices fall.'

Europe's top banks are down in the dumps. And that is putting the case lightly. Deutsche Bank's share went down lower than its recession price. Standard Chartered's share price is at its lowest in nearly 20 years.

The Swiss bank Credit Suisse stock was down 43 percent over the last year and touched a 27-year low. If Credit Suisse tries to sell their bonds they will get junk rates. Their trading income is abysmal.

In UK, HSBC, Lloyds, Barclays and RBS tell a similar story.

Falling off a cliff. Since the beginning of 2016, the Stoxx Europe 600 Banks Index, has lost 27 per cent.

If you had invested in banks a decade ago you would have not made a profit. That was in Feb 2016. By Nov 2016 you would have made a loss.

After 2008 the economy in developed countries was not exciting. So banks turned to emerging Asian and African economies providing them eight years of easy money. But borrowers are struggling,

Now, increasingly, borrowers in millions don't have the money to repay.

The problem with banks is — they ask you to take a loan and then they want you to pay it back whether you have the money or not.

Was there any forecast. Any sort of analysis? Could the banks not even foresee the effect of providing money at a flow? Banks have created a bubble that will burst in their face.

Watch Deutsche stock price reach single digit. Pathetic.

The credit default swap (CDS) of Deutsche has risen to high levels. This means that the cost of insuring against a default by Deutsche has risen considerably.

Flashback 2008: Remember the banks which fell. Some of them never got up. Be careful which bank you put your money.

The moon is a safe place. There are no banks on the moon.

They will drive you mad, the banks. Banks will go down and they will take with them everything else.

Why does common sense get the kick when it comes to managing global economy?

The European Central Bank (ECB) increases its very own quantitative easing, piling on public debt to the private debt it has already accumulated. The ECB has planned to increase its QE from €14 billion to €60 billion until at least September of 2016.

It has failed in US. It has failed in Japan. Still the ECB is at it. This will only create a spiral of problems. It will act as a multiplier of economic dangers.

Clever people learn from others mistakes, fools from their own and idiots never.

The more you blow a bubble the bigger it gets. The bigger a bubble balloon the louder it will burst.

ECB is blowing the cash bubble. More and more. Harder and harder. The bigger it gets the worse will be the explosion.

It's all about the banks in Europe. Seven of the top 10 distressed banks are in Europe. It will be a rout of the likes unseen. And perhaps it may well begin with Deutsche.

The US Justice department has sent out a notice. A notice of 14 billion dollar fine relating to a case of mortgage security sale fraud. And the market value of Deutsche bank is only 16 billion dollars. It holds less than 3% of assets as capital.

A quagmire of banks in a cesspool.

Nov 2016: French PM 'Europe on the brink of collapse.'

Europe Lives In Delusion...

The Gulf Deficit

Oil. It seems fantasy that oil costed more than 100 dollars just a couple of years back. When it touched 40 the venerable sheiks wished that was the bottom.

They survive on oil. And oil will never bounce back to those heady days.

The technology for drilling is making the cost of drilling out oil less and lesser.

Moreover the era of oil is over. Done and oiled.

Humanity has to look ahead, look elsewhere. One day or the other, oil had to be exhausted. We discovered engines and invented modern ways to use oil just a 100 - 150 years ago. In the span of human history this is like a blip click. But we have used oil as much as we could and overheated the globe in the process. Life is transient. Hard luck.

In 2015, its budget deficit nearly reached $ 100 billion. Now, Saudi Arabia is looking for an $8 billion loan. Headcounts are being lowered. Cost cutting which was once unthinkable in the gulf countries is becoming policy.

In 2016 six of the rich Arab economies planned to borrow upto $20 billion. Till now they were the lenders to the world. Now they are planned borrowers. This is the state of affairs when oil touched 40. And it is likely oil will be below 40 forever.

And these have nil else to prop their economy as of now. The venerable sheiks have put all their eggs in the oil basket. It is only now they have realized this and are making attempts to diversify. But that will take time to happen.

After a long fight within themselves the OPEC has finally in October 2016 agreed to decrease oil output by a million barrels a day. It is a bit of an upside for oil prices and to their economies. From 33 million barrels a day to 32 million barrels a day. And just 2 weeks later the entire agreement has come unhinged. Every OPEC member is playing for himself. There is a see-saw among the OPEC members who decide and then undecide. Russia a non-OPEC member has increased its output and agrees for a freeze. No decrease from Russia, a freeze at current levels. And oil continues its downward journey after a brief pause.

In the longer term, oil is an exhaustible energy source. Alternative energies are the future of civilization. Governments the world over are promoting alternative energies. Technology is gaining. We have had Solar Impulse make a round the world trip with not a drop of gasoline. West Asia the hub of oil and gas has itself been making a shift to solar energy production lately. If we get to air travel on alternative energy that will be the end of oil as the major source of transport energy that connects existence.

Countries have to reduce carbon imprints. Clean energy is a must for survival of the globe.

Humans are done with oil. It is written in the sky in carbon. The era of oil is over.

One era to another. We have to be on the move.

The Gulf Widens...

Asia In Doldrums

Feb 2016

News: Has Japan's grand attempt to reflate the world's third largest economy failed? The Bank of Japan (BOJ) crossed over into uncharted territory, pushing interest rates below zero for the first time ever.

For the first time ever.

In just two days in Feb-2016 the Japanese stock market was down nearly 8%. The GDP figures indicated that the Japanese economy was shrinking again.

There is a strange problem in Japan where large corporations are sitting of piles of cash - as much as 3 trillion. But are not spending it. Because they are afraid their investment will not get returns in the current and the foreseeable future. The Japan businessmen know for sure the economy is on a major downswing.

Hold on to dear money !

Exports in Asian giants Japan, China and South Korea drop by double digits.

Asia In Doldrums...

ETHICS IN BUSINESS

An ancient saying - Even robbers have ethics. What about businessmen and bankers?

Some executives are known to take hundreds of millions of dollars in bonuses. Executives live the high life and we know some buy islands for them to frolick around. I have nil against that provided it is all well earned (and not by insider trading). And shared.

I am sure you have heard of Rajaratinam and his elite network that made it a cakewalk for him to indulge in insider trading and super profits in short time. Some are notoriously brilliant and the rest of us follow the rules. I have heard of his insider trading but have not as yet heard of him sharing a wee bit of his wealth. That might have made him a Robin Hood of sorts! Rajaratinam is in jail alongwith with Rajat who one time was with McKinsey Consulting.

The biggest problem with capitalism is cronyism. The top 'leadership' rakes it in and in times of crisis more often than not the buck stops at the lower levels. The top protect each other and take millions in bonuses, equity and whatever.

Like in Wells Fargo where its own customers were given accounts they didn't need and charged money for transactions that were not required. The guys at the bottom are being blamed. And not a single guy who took in those millions was aware of what was happening behind their bottoms? Incredible. Rip off your own customers and take not a shred of the blame.

If you don't share you go down. One more time nature will teach us this lesson in 2016-2018.

Yet again. Yet one more time.

Spread the wealth. To the have nots. The cosmos means business. And we all better listen.

When corporates made super profits did they give it back not only to their shareholders but stakeholders and the community in equal measure? Actually, it is economic common sense and doesn't need an MBA to figure out that money spread over a population, goes around and keeps the engines of a community humming. Concentrated in a few hands it is useless.

When banks offered you loans did they eye only their own chart busting profits? There is a problem when banks rush in and give loans. No matter what.

When big corporates showed signs of default were they categorized as such in the balance sheet or were they hidden under some accounting jargon. Which means when the banks showed profit they were actually in loss. Did they hide it?

When large corporates defaulted were the loans collected or worse were more loans offered. This is a problem not endemic to Asia as we thought. Though it is changing there as well. Some big fish use whatever rules, laws and clauses or hidden text. Or shift their money to tax havens. And some small fish caught in the EMI net struggle. To break free.

Isn't there a wide gap between the so many so many people who just about earn and just have just enough and those who are very rich. In the USA there is vast number of people who are not satisfied about their salaries. There is a clear divide between the rich and the rest.

Cornerstone Macro technical analyst Carter Worth told CNBC's "Fast Money" traders. "When you see the relative performance of utilities, bonds and the S&P 500 index acting opposite to each other, you're about to get another contraction."

The correlation between these three factors as well as gold and corporate bonds was analyzed. Carter stated that each divergence and contraction took place during periods of recession.

Not only has he predicted a deep recession but goes on to say: "It's very hard to reverse it."

Economic destiny is a pet theme of this book.

'The results of every action are etched at the time of the action itself.'

The world's best are trying all they can and more. Every trick and every tactic. And find that it all spills up in their faces.

Economics is destiny.

Destiny puts you in your place. If you have done right you will be in the right place. If you have done wrong you will be in the wrong place. I hope you have been ethical while earning your money. Because destiny has a way of catching up.

The FDA has fined 14 billion dollars to Deutsche bank for mortgage security fraud.

Wells Fargo rips off its own customers. And is facing the music possibly a class action suit?

One fraud after another. By someone we trust.

Will Deutsche Bank be the Lehman Bros of 2016?

At the time we decide we need to decide right. At the time we act we need to act right.

THE ARMAGEDDON

Global economics is global destiny.

Central banks are running 'out of ammunition'.

CNN Money 9 Feb 2016

'They're pumping money into their economies, creating negative interest rates and buying billions of dollars in bonds. Yet experts are worried these strategies will not be enough to turn around the slump in the world.'

"As soon as the markets realize that the Fed and the ECB are out of ammunition, it's over," Stockman said. "I think we're in an extremely unsafe world — we've never been here before."

This is by a former US government Director of Budget.

'We are getting into a place where we have never been before.'

The Armageddon.

VOODOO ECONOMICS

They are manufacturing cash out of thin air. The voodoo economists.

It failed in Japan and it failed in USA. Yet the ECB is gung ho about it.

QE1 was useful. We should have bitten the bullet then. QE2 and QE3 were largely pumping money that was used to create a sense of well being. Like being on steroids.

The more the delay the more the spread of the cancer. The cancer has spread to all over. If the Fed does the surgery the patient may die on the operating table. So they continue to make the patient feel that all is well. Until he is alive.

We the common people are the patient. You and I. The common folks. The surgeons know it. That is the economists and the guys in the central banks. They know the cancer has spread all over the global economy.

And we are staring at best a recession while all indicators actually point towards a depression.

The great depression of 2017. Big banks will collapse like ninepins. Stock markets across the globe will swing down faster than you can react, bonds too. The most valued investment across the world, real estate, will go up in smoke.

THE BABY BOOMERS – OUT OF ACTION

In 1989 Japan reached the height of its economy. Today Japan is just another lagging economy trying to find its bearings. It's home to an ageing economically inactive population.

USA today is facing a similar issue. The disappearance of the baby boomer generation – the bulk of its generation driving the economy – buying, investing and entrepreneuing. In the USA this generation controls 4 times the GDP of its country. It's these economically active people, actually an economic powerhouse that were responsible for the greatest economic activity through the 70's, 80's and 90's; that are entering into retirement hibernation. A major chunk of peak household spending is going to go out. The US government states 'This will have a profound economic effect.' It's simple – People are at the core of the economy; people move the economy.

THE CYCLES PREDICT A CRASH

Corporates need to forecast downward graphs. We can't keep going up all the time. The economy moves in cycles. Study of the cyclical trends of modern economic history should be the baseline for every management executive. The reasons for the ebb and flow of modern economy has to be analyzed and the rise and fall has to be factored in. The cyclical trends are a powerful means of prediction and knowing the events likely to happen will put decision making back in human hands rather than let us be overwhelmed by random events that coalesce to form a tsunami.

The discoverer of the K waves was executed because he predicted the end of certain type of civilization decades before it actually fell apart.

The K waves. The K wave predicts a recession in 2017. Other cycles of economy for instance the 8.6 year cycle (the last recession was in 2008) converge to the same year. Cyclical theories too coalesce to the year 2017. And that is unnerving.

During the great depression of 1929 people lost homes, the rich became poor, millions had to stand in soup lines just to survive.

During the stock market crash of 1987 23% value was lost in a single day. And that was not even a recession.

As of November 2016, 19 of the 28 European countries are in huge debt. 30 banks in Europe have stocks that are trading at historic lows. These include the global big banks like Soceite General, Paribas and Santander.

Japan's debt is 2.5 times its GDP. And worse, nobody is investing money knowing that they may not get it back.

Negative interest rates in some countries. You have to pay the bank to keep your money.

The USA has not seen deflation since the Great Depression. After the fiasco of QE has the Fed succeeded in stoking inflation? They intend to raise interest rates once they hit their inflation target. They have been waiting since Feb-2016. Agonizing wait.

The debtpile of the US government keeps growing with social security and the mediaid and medicare bills. It will cross $20 trillion and that will be a milestone of sorts.

Once Euro and Japan crash, the wealthy there will try to shift their money to USA. The stocks will rise. But only just. It's panic money. The USA too will not be able to sustain the huge influx because the fundamentals will not support. And the markets will crash. First a rise in US stocks followed by a mighty fall. This is one of the scenarios how it might play out.

Warren Buffet has 55 billion dollars in cash. That is the most cash he has in 40 years. Why has he not invested in the market?

George Soros has increased his short position 5 times.

Jim Rogers says he is staying away from the US stockmarket.

These are the 3 legends of investing this century. Their actions tell just one story : The markets are going to go down.

It's about time too. From 2009, 8 years of bull market (Much of it though is by way of dubious 'easy' money.)

The worry that the flood of cash has encouraged needless risky financial decisions is real. And the result of this easy money on emerging economies is an illusion.

Illusion of cash. Illusion of investment. Illusion of economy.

We have created an illusionary global economy. The real economy is uncomfortable with illusions. Its basic nature is to get back to reality. Sooner or later.

Watch out for 2017. It will be the year when QE will be stopped globally. And the economy attempts to get back to reality with a crash.

2017 : The Coming Crash.

THE RESULTS

The results can be read in the preparation. What you will be is in exponential proportion to what you do now.

You can judge the action by the result. And the result by the action.

Glance at the 2016 results. What horrendous decisions over the last decade has led to these results ?

Venezuela: 720 % inflation

Greece: Debt Crisis

Spain: Debt Crisis

Italy: A banking cesspool

China debt to GDP: 260%

USA: QE Bubble

Japan: Negative interest rates

Saudis: Lenders turn borrowers

The breadth of bad economic news spans the globe. From one end to another. With only a few islands of relief. These will also get dragged into the connected quagmire.

The stark landscape of history is a pointer to this immutable law.

From Goliath who fell to Lehmann bros which vanished. Deutsche bank is much bigger than Lehmann Bros whose collapse in led to the 2008 recession.

Warren Buffet calls Derivatives 'Weapons of Mass Destruction'. They are known to be extremely toxic and can bring down banks like nothing else. And Deutsche has $46 trillion of these. The illiquid asset is $10 billion. Worse, the actual value of its assets is a mystery. It may be much below its shown book value. Deutsche bank had has put its subsidiary on the block. But nobody is willing to buy a Deutsche subsidiary.

An Italian court has slapped charges on Deutsche Bank over its role in covering up and falsifying Italy's oldest bank Monte Paschi losses and mistrades. The USA DOJ has slapped $ 16 billion fine.

More than all these Deutsche bank is heavily networked with several prominent banks. If it goes down it will take a few others too along with it. The stock price of Deutsche is below its 2008 recession price. And the grand top-up is that Deutsche bank is struggling to earning profit.

This time, will Deutsche bank will be the first of the big banks to collapse. And others will follow?

In 2008 it was the recession. This time will it be the depression?

A stitch in time saves nine. The time has passed. Will the nine survive 2017? But the stitch didn't happen in time....

SPECULATION

Speculation is the opposite of utility. If you gain 100 today you might as well lose 1000 tomorrow. There is no logic to speculation. Event based decisions are not speculations.

There is a mythic story of a dice game between two rival kings vying for the same kingdom. As the game of dice progresses the innocent and good king overwhelmed by the game keeps upping the stake until he pledges his kingdom. And he loses the throw of the dice and his kingdom!

Speculation since historical times has been bringing down men, families, populations and kingdoms.

Will the speculative trades in stocks or the big banks speculative coverage including derivatives contribute to bring down the global order of economy in 2017? All it takes is a couple of big reversals and the speculative positions will fall with a domino effect. A pack of cards.

The throw of dice has already been done. And I know the result. By now you would too!

Nobody has ever won a kingdom by speculation. Since mythic times.

Derivatives are official casinos. They are bets and are speculative. They are 7 times the size of global economy.

UTILITY

Availability of cash created an economy which did not have real utility. People created coz they had money not coz they had use or need for it. So you had ghost cities. Which fuelled a ghost economy and people didn't know of it until it became a ghostly news story.

The last trick was QE. QE was useful initially. In large part the QE had outlived its utility. Did the central banks carry out an analysis of the utility of QE every six months or every year?

No. They just had a blind shot.

But from now on the Cosmos will put utility on center stage. Right up there.

The fetal cities of China. The 'city planners', the 'masters of economy' the false creations of the commodity boom, the exports boom in several countries. The unborn cities will ring in the death knell of the modern mismanaged economy. We should not build cities that will not be populated. Violation of the crucial economic principle: Utility.

Do something useful that will be used.

A fitness program that promotes health.

A preacher who is sincere.

A banker who gives a loan which gives ROI.

A clinical research which results in a drug that cures.

A goldsmith who crafts a design which is aesthetic.

A builder who designs a city which is smart.

An economist whose policy alleviates poverty.

A leader who implements.

A movie that people enjoy to watch.

An assassination which is globally applauded.

All these have utility. They are useful. They can be used.

People will flock to us even in a recession.

Why do I say all this? It seems to be pretty obvious. But much happens in the world that on hindsight seems so very foolish.

More than a 1000 clinical trials were recently rejected due to dubious data. We all know of leaders who never implement. We have seen movies which we didn't enjoy. We have had wars which didn't serve a purpose.

While in theory doing right, doing well and doing the best seems to be just natural; in reality we find decisions and events can be downright gross.

So if we are the ones who stand up and in whatever domain we are in we can justly say I am of utility (quality, consistency, expertise, knowledge, information and delivery) people will flock to us even in a recession.

Do our world leaders and economist and bankers need to be taught this basic lesson of human economic behavior — Utility?

In our frenzy a penchant has grown, a temptation to make the simple convoluted. Making life complicated we have tied ourselves in a complex web that we are unable to get out of. Risky complicated derivatives and other financial products so convoluted that we just don't get it.

The more the convoluted the more the genius?

Actually the more seamlessly simple it seems, the more the genius.

A genius simplifies the complex.

E = MC Square.

Simple. Utility.

The Survival Guide.

Finally we are here. What can you do? As individuals. Because governments will not be able to do much. In fact may not be able to do anything at all.

Here are some solutions, some measures that you can pick and choose. Choose the best options. The ones that suit you, that make sense to you.

Here we go.

What should I Do? I.

"Only I can Act. Now."

1. Skill yourself: Make yourself useful and more useful at whatever level you are in. Get that much better. Domain skill, technical skill, networking skill, service skill, communication skill...Do right to yourself. Then do right

to your community. Then you might find yourself in the right place when you meet catastrophe face to face.

2. Compact: One Person Business. If you can manage a business alone then you can float. Use tech, use e-comm, use gadgets. That will cut down cost of employees (you can take home the salary of every person you don't employee). And using online somewhere can possibly cut down on realty space.

3. Family Business: The profit goes to the family.

4. Cost: Can you service a demand at lesser cost. Obviously cost will be a significant determinant. Right on top.

5. Practice agriculture. You will be assured of food, housing and health. The small farm house. Being with nature and working on the farm is as healthy as it can get. And food can be a business.

Agriculture is one of Jim Rogers favorite. Mine too. In fact this can be one of the most safest and even profitable if you can think of it in that way during a crisis.

6. Urban planting.

Use LED light as a substitute for sunlight. LED plants require 10 times less space and but give a high yield.

Soiless planting. Mineralized water that supply just the minerals that are need. No soil.

So there, in a small space you have all the nutritious food you would ever want. It may not matter if the sun rises the next day or not.

You may start a home delivery of essential food.

7. Community: This is vital. Be a vibrant community. Just don't look at the size. The community has to be vibrant. The support system.

WhatsApp with an extended live ecosystem. That will keep your spirits afloat and high. We cannot just survive we can live during a recession! The colors of a community become our colors. Be a prominent part of a community of common as well as strategic interests.

8. Gold. One of Wall Street's most accurate forecasters JP Morgan's Kolanovic predicts that stocks markets are in trouble. His choice of investment is gold.

The CEO of Euro Pacific Capital says the U.S. economy is in the midst of a recession that could turn out to be even more horrible than the Great Recession of 2008. He is confident of only this option: Gold. The safe haven. But buy on dips. And no asset is up forever. You also need to know when to get out.

It does make sense however to keep a portion of investment in different asset classes.

Why gold? Instinctively we all will rush for it.

Go For Gold. Buy on dips.

9. But some experts plump for dollars. Their advice is to purchase dollars. Betting for Dollars against other currencies.

Jim Rogers buys into dollars not because it has inherent strength but because lot of people believe it to be strong and will buy it. Or it may be the only one of the few options available when all else is sinking. A place to stay put for sometime.

10. Stocks, bonds (other than inflation linked bonds), real estate, oil will be down.

11. Place. Where you will be, stay and earn will matter the most.

If you wish to stay reasonable by the end of 2017 then plan to head to the few places in the world that are relatively untouched.

UNESCO has voted him the best PM in the world. India. This country has rallied behind one of the few world leaders worth his salt. Who says what he means and means what he says. Backed by the governor of their central bank they have one of the fastest real growths currently. They are investing in roads, trains and housing.

Indonesia. Or the few such countries. South East Asia.

12. If you can't head there then consider investing in some Asian economies.

Asia Focused Funds (AFF). Get in touch with them. Seek out the financial data of the country. Compare the financial parameters and Invest.

Debt, Debt to GDP ratio, Growth Rate. The basics will give an idea.

Seek out sectors and companies that profit from internal business.

Check for companies that are focused on emerging core technologies and emerging technologies.

Spread your investment among sectors and companies.

Even such financial indicators as EPS and PE can give a fair idea of the companies you plan to invest in. If you want to dig deeper you can go into debt-equity ratio, percentage of other income in the profit, project orders in hand and so on.

The way you invest and manage will be different. Ask your financial advisor some pointed questions. If you see him squirm then maybe you asked him right.

But do enquire about upcoming investment and projects. Biosimilars, robotics, electric cars, renewable energy, cloud computing, data analytics, e-com, VR, digital and so on. Online ventures and AI startups before you know can be all over the place. What is happening now and in the near future. Mix the current and the future (current and future profit). Go for it.

13. Lithium the 'fuel' of electric cars. And graphene. The new age wonder. These can take off. That is obvious.

14. As per a recent survey people who live in Denmark, Norway, Sweden and Switzerland are the happiest in the world. Don't worry. Be happy. Head to Holland.

Escape. It's a chance to have an adventure.

Escape to happy countries.

Immigrate.

15. Stay in A Forest. Yes. This is a serious option. Deep in the forest. Or near habitation. In a tree house. Make it safe whichever you choose. You can live out your fantasies. And you may have the best time of your life. An adventure you only dreamed about.

16. Hobby. Take up that hobby that you always dreamt of and you many find a treasure within yourself. Now that you may have time. Don't think about ROI for this year. See how liberating that can be. By the way have you heard of Charles Darrow and a hobby? Read on.

17. Write a diary. It can be a surprising perspective a side of yourself you didn't know existed. Some diaries have gone on to become bestsellers. The grit the survival the pleasures and happiness even in the adversity the enduring spirit of human life.

18. SSP : Did ever your financial advisor tell you about SSP. The Systematic Selling Plan?

Horse with blinkers. Many a times education makes us see only what we have been trained to. It makes us blind to the reality which is all around us.

In Feb 2016 the stocks were down. In Oct 2016 the stocks again went down. Over the course of next year there will be global sell off. Or at the very least, times when the stocks will be down.

If you sell systematically every time the stocks rise, you can pick them at a lower price when the stocks go down or you can book the profit and watch it go down all the way.

Warren Buffet has $ 55 billion in cash. What about you?

Start Now.

Were there no rich people during the great depression of 1929 and were there no one who became rich due to the depression ?

It's not only about survival. Getty became a Rockfeller only because of the great depression. It can open up unseen possibilities — Be alert to ever changing scenario. Get ready for the roller coaster ride. And if you make the right decisions at the right time you will end on the top of the wave. If you think we are talking only money here then you are dead wrong.

We are talking of life. And there is more to life than just money.

Read on.

People will just prefer to celebrate the forest life or write a diary of this rare time of 201;, some will downright be focused on the funds the SSP and the AFF and others will mix and match the options such as community and home agri and make it a part of their lifestyle.

Whatever you choose to do, it is about time you start.

The better prepared cope better.

The King and His Preacher.

Let me tell you the story of a king who invited his preacher for a hunt. Armed with bows, arrows and spears the huntsmen enter the forest. Deep inside the dense forest amidst large gnarled trees and thick creepers the sounds of the wild keep the huntsmen on the alert. After he has had his turn, the king points towards boar and offers the preacher a gilded bow and arrow.

"Go for it good preacher."

The preacher says "Your Kingship. I am a preacher.

 What would I know about hunting?"

The King replies "Try your luck good preacher. Who knows you might get it just right. The Bulls Eye. Ha, Ha."

The preacher moves back, tries to position himself as he can and let's go. It's pure disaster.

The arrow has gone haywire and has pierced the king's arm.

Angered by this the king orders the preacher to the dungeons while he himself driven by a royal thirst for adventure carries on with the hunt.

But then, there is danger lurking around the corner. A downswing in the life of the king. Cannibals await their next meal and the king walks right into the cannibal tribe while many of his soldiers escape into the wilderness.

Just as they are about to fry the king one of them notices the open gash on the kings arm. Afraid of bad omen they refuse to consider the king as food and release him.

The king rushes back to his palace, heads to the dungeons and hugs the preacher.

"Good preacher. If you had not injured me with the misaimed arrow and had I not this wound on my arm the cannibals would have found me to be perfect and would have fried me in burning oil. Thanks to you, I am alive today!"

"Your Kingship. Had you not put me in the dungeons I would have still accompanied you. The cannibals finding me without any injury would have selected me as their food. Thanks to you, I am alive today!"

A downswing in our lives. We may get hurt maybe even badly but then it may be for the good. I am sure it can be if we take some sensible steps.

Limpid Eyed Cosmos

I had a bit cosmos hugging me today. Looking at me with limpid eyes. I was carrying her. She will save me from the harsh world. My 2 year girl going onto 3. Just about making sense of the world. But not touched by it. Hug your own cosmos, support them; they will be your saviors. When you look at their expectant innocent eyes and face you get a sense of belongingness. Yes we belong to someone. That is the essence of our existence.

But then we will need to look beyond those who belong to us. Just in case we have forgotten in the hurry to reach our targets.

Our targets will now reach as low as they can get and give us all the time we need to learn that interwoven is our life and we need to reach out to every human we come across in as natural a manner that nature ordained human behavior to be.

It seems apt to end where it all began. Targets.

What is your target? 'Your.'

What is the target of humanity? 'Humanity'.

You achieve your targets.

And allow humanity to achieve its.

What is humanity's target. Money, business, profit at any cost ?

Humane. Be humane. All the time. At any meet. At any conference. Any decision. Every pitch. Every tactic. Every strategy.

Be humane.

The End Result.

Generate profit at any cost ? "Ha Ha."

Success Stories

Darrow : Driven out of work by the great depression Charles Darrow spent time in designing a game that went on to be called Monopoly. It became so popular that the first ever game designer millionaire was created.

Getty : He inherited 5,00,000 dollars. When the stocks crashed he bought oil stocks at their lowest level. J Paul Getty held on for a long enough time to become the first billionaire of the great depression.

Kennedy: Joe Kennedy made his money in the stock market and got out at the right times to invest in real estate and movie studios to stay rich for more time.

You can become rich in the stock market. But to stay rich you need to know when to get out. Get out before the others do.

Cullen : Cullen worked in the retail market. He gave an idea that his bosses rejected. He went out on a limb and worked out his idea that ultimately made him 75 million dollars.

You have an idea you believe in. Recessions and depressions are just great times to work out ideas that have been rejected.

Cagney: James Cagney went from $500 to $40000 a week. Depressions have been extremely fertile ground for creatives. Legends have been born.

What are you waiting for?

As the man who pulverized the great depression of 1929 famously said : 'You have only fear to fear.' FDR.

It's not only about the money, baby.

Script Your Success.

THE REVIVAL

And when it does revive as it will, the cataclysmic changes will be akin to the metamorphosis of a caterpillar into a butterfly.

In the early 1900 those who were affluent had iceboxes. A horse drawn carriage would stop by to deliver ice everyday. Until refrigerators were invented. Not long back the night was lit by lamps until electricity was discovered. Civilization changed. Time was when letters took days to reach your feelings to your loved ones. SMS does it in an instant. Reality seemed magical.

Our children will live in a world they did not grow up in. Drones, hyperloop speed, personalized gene based medical therapy, anti-ageing, robots, facial recognition, chatbots, flying cars (yes they will come much before self driving cars), virtual reality and technology that will once again change the screen saver of history and make the world so different than it was ever before.

Humankind will emerge once again.

The Last Word

That economy which circulates within reasonable limits spikes within reasonable limits. And the economy which crosses all limits crashes without limit.

It will start with the interest rate hike. Stocks will crash. Real estate will join in.

It will start when the QE ends.

It will start with banks. Deutsche? Taking down Italy, Spain, Greece spreading like a contagion through Europe, Japan. USA has its own set of issues that are enough and interconnected for it to fall like never before witnessed in the history of humans.

The great recession of 2017 is staring at us.

It is right here.

The Last Thoughts

The indicators are the result.

Be humane. Don't rip off your own customers.

Zero interest rate regimes has led to over-production.

A consumption not driven by need contributes to the formation of a bubble.

To escape the effects of the 2008 QE was started. Pump in easy money. With no real demand. By not withdrawing QE and taking their medicine in 2012 – market imbalances today are now bigger and the consequences greater.

The culprits are the central banks (though they are not the only ones). This is where they started giving cash to create the cash illusion.

15 Nov 2016. French PM: "Europe on brink of Collapse"

Search for places to hide. To escape the avalanche of the economic holocaust.

Live at the fringe. Get the best of both the worlds.

Live at the fringe. Get the best of the forest and get away from the worst of the city.

It will begin with the banks. And extend everywhere.

Uninvest to Reinvest.

Trump. Trade wars And The Great Fall Of China.

Chinese real estate magnate Wang Jianlin has stated that "Residential real estate in China is now the biggest bubble in history." One prick and the blast will wipe off a third of GDP.

Torsten Slok who works as a chief international economist has a chart which shows that China's credit bubble exceeded even that of USA on the edge of subprime mortgage meltdown that led into the 2008 recession.

The coming crash will be worse than a recession.

We will have ample time to think about this as the events unfold before our seemingly unbelieving eyes.

The culprits are the banks. They give 'easy' money. And expect it back.

Did the banks think that people will borrow from them and make profits out of a tentative economy? And pay them back for the banks to enjoy super profits! How dreamy! Or delusional?

Did we talk about executives who own islands while there are millions who rent a shelter on a day basis. The haves and the have nots. Is this all about this?

Are we the destined witness of an Economic Holocaust?

It is nature's way of purging excess and dead sloth greed from its system. Nature and the real economy don't like these.

The moon is a safe place. I will go there. Because there are no banks on the moon.

We have a downswing. Look up. Someone up there may know what he is doing. Read 'The King And The Preacher'.

QE: When everything fails we fall back on magic. Close your eyes. Open now. Hey we have more money! The voodoo economics of the voodoo economists.

The stats are staggeringly negative.

Be brave and bite the bullet. We should have. The last chance was missed.

The End Result is an extrapolation of the initial decision multiplied by a factor.

The End Result is Upon Us. Wait and Watch. Or Get Out. Fast.

This time the recession will teach us to be humane.

To purge the wild excesses, the panicky decisions, the irrational behavior, the greedy clinging and the selfish motivations and cowardly attitude.

The precision of the universe is at play.

Forget the community; forget the climate; forget the have nots. Let's just achieve targets. "Ha.Ha."

Nature and Humaneness will together have the last laugh. "Ha.Ha."

When the indicators are bad the result cannot be good.

Economic indicators are like health indicators. When you have a bad lab test then surely there must be a bad disease that led to it.

Indicators are precursors of results. We can't have bad indicators and a good result. We can't have increased troponins and wish that the heart is normal. Right now the global economic indicators are the worst in 3 decades. Expect to have the worst recession in the past 30-50 years.

When the indicators are bad the result will be bad. And right now the indicators are very very very bad.

Marks And Spencer shuts down a 100 stores. A 100...!!!

Global economy is global destiny.

Lots of people not employed. Lots of people with less salary. Lots of people with less savings. Lots of people with more expenses. Lots of people on the other side. Lots of have nots. USA Today.

Sometimes the best comes out of the worst. Hope that we are in that situation.

Utilize every moment. These will never come back.

What we have been doing is against humanity's target. And there lies the crux of the problem and the biggest lesson the Cosmos is trying to teach us though the coming crash.

There is Life beyond ROI.

Government may have been the reason for the recession? Because they bailed out the big banks with public money. And big banks created a speculative bubble of derivates 30 times the size of the US debt — more than $ 500 trillion of derivatives.

Banks or casinos?

When banks become casinos the economy is a gamble.

A must read for everyone to know how the global economy arrived at the mess it is in.

HSBC has issued a red alert on stocks.

A small spark starts a jungle fire when the twigs are dry and many.

Basically it is about the basics. Basics are the foundation. Basics are the building blocks. Basics are all there is. Basic is the end point.

You get the basic right you get everything right.

You decide your future at the time you act.

Useful plus Used = Effective.

The next two years will reveal that utility is linked to survival.

Charles Darwin's Survival of the Fittest will be successfully tested once again.

Someone who is skilled is always of value. Those who are useful will be used. And will be paid for the use.

Even in a recession people will visit a restaurant that serves tasty nutritious food, to watch that movie which is entertaining and go to that doctor who gives accurate diagnosis.

Compact: This will make a strong comeback.

Many big banks will have to withdraw to survive. And shed to become lean. Smaller banks will survive and thrive.

Compact and utility will go hand in hand.

Will we witness a recession, depression or holocaust?

Warren Buffet has a name for derivatives. He calls them Weapons of Mass Destruction.

Be ready for fly by wire decisions.

There will be minimal government intervention. Coz governments have done all they could. And have no more tricks in the bag.

Until the revival we have to fend for ourselves and the decision making starts now.

One step in the right direction gives the strength for two steps in the right direction. Two steps in the right direction gives the strength for 4 steps in the right direction. 4 steps... Just substitute the word right with wrong and see where you end up.

1929 Lets go back and take a look.

In the great depression of 1929 were there no rich people. Yet for every wealthy guy every there were thousands holding the food bowl.

Where do you want to be in 2017. How to get to where you want to be in 2017.

Make a decision based on facts. Take a considered opinion.

Belongingness gives us the strength to carry on against all odds. The more we enlarge our belongingness the more humane we will be.

It's a game. The game is on. It can affect. It's real. Play it well. It is not static.

Be alert.

Situations will be dynamic.

Subscribe to read.

Spend at least 10 mins a day to watch targeted news.

Get alerts to your Whatsapp.

Timing is crucial. High stakes games. Very crucial.

Small steps but big stakes!

Whatsapp for entertainment. Now use Whatsapp for the game of your life. Join or create a group. Get real time news and flashes.

We cannot just survive we can live during a recession! The colors of a community become our colors.

Have a meaningful conversation with your financial advisor. Ask and engage him.

Sell stocks. If you don't want to do it all at once, the other option is to do it with a SSP.

Everytime your stocks go up. Download. So that you get the best average price. But start now.

The situation will be dynamic. It is important to know when to buy and more important to know when to sell.

Hobby. We can discover facets to life hitherto hidden. That can be fascinating. And you can be the Charles Darrow of 2017!

Forest — Nature. We can discover facets to life hitherto hidden. That can be fascinating.

If you are in profit it is time to download stocks now. Systematic Selling Plan.

Follow the legends.

Warren Buffet has the most cash uninvested in the market.

Jim Rogers intends to buy dollars

George Soros has increased his short positions

Accumulate the safe haven metals on dips. Lithium is the new and spectacular 'precious metal' and on the other end is gold the perennial safe haven. Consider graphene – the new kid on the block.

Focus on South Asian funds

Immigrate to happy countries

Reach out to me

More millionaires were made during the great depression than at other times.

Happiness is a byproduct of attitude. Improve your attitude.

Imagine the time when there were no cities. We lived in the forest. We lived.

When Greece collapsed the banks in Greece were closed. People had to line up at ATMs for their daily ration of fixed money.

A survivor said : Parents dream for their kids. I live a nightmare and see my children foraging garbage for food.

Stay at the fringe of a forest where the city ends. And the recession can be an adventure in a tree house. And you can live.

Get the best of air, water and fruits and enter the city to do what you have to do. But come back to the fringe where the city meets the forest. For this is the place where ... you can live.

You won't need electricity because the moonlight will be there to take care of you and all that you wear.

THE LAST QUOTES

"I would liken the Fed to a blindfolded arsonist. Armed, dangerous and lost." The former director of the Office of Management and Budget, Stockman. Stockman has been a lynchpin of the US government during its heydays.

"As soon as the markets realize that the Fed and the ECB are out of ammunition, it's over." Stockman.

"I think we're in an extremely unsafe world — we've never been here before." Stockman.

"Whoever replaces Barack Obama is going to inherit a worse recession than the one that he inherited from Bush." Schiff.

"A lot of the problems in the investment bank have been that people have been trying to generate revenue at all costs." Thiam, CEO Credit Suisse.

Generate revenue at any cost. "Ha Ha."- Piam, Publisher.

The Last Minute

IN 2017

ECONOMICS WILL MAKE HISTORY

THE REVIVAL.

Graphene. Bend anything.

Anti-ageing drugs. Live young forever.

Flying cars. Fly away.

Bye To All.

Be Someone @The Revival.

THE TECH SHIFT

BY PIAM

2016 @ AMAZON * CREATESPACE

www.gipv.net

THE ADVENTURES OF THE ORANCZ TRIANGLEZ

PIAM CREATIONS

ANIMATION FILM @ 2017

You Want To Produce A Film : pi.con.publisher@gmail.com

"IN THE WOMB OF THE END LIES A NEW BEGINNING."

PIAM.

www.ingramcontent.com/pod-product-compliance
Lightning Source LLC
Chambersburg PA
CBHW070107210526
45170CB00013B/774